Embrace the Holiday Spirit

A Chorus of Baahs, Buzzes, Pecks, and Purrs

Embrace the Holiday Spirit

A Chorus of Baahs, Buzzes, Pecks, and Purrs

Judith Shenouda,
Kerry Roberts, and
Julia Ward

Shenouda Associates Inc.
Pittsford, NY, USA

Creative design and editorial services by Shenouda Associates Inc.

Shenouda Associates Inc.

Pittsford, NY, USA

ISBN-13: 978-1-7322223-7-3
ISBN-10: 1-7322223-7-3

Contents

Dedication

This book is dedicated to the babies, the toddlers, the youngsters, the mature, and the many-seasoned seniors who are reading or listening to the stories and quotes, looking at the photographs, and feasting on the treats made from the recipes provided in these pages. May your every day be a holiday rightly guided to a place and space of awe and wonder in the spirit of the season.

Cast of Critters

Anty Annie the Ant

Baby Chick Chick, Fuzzy Chick Chick, and Papa

Belle Birdie and Bobalong Bird

Bumbler B, Honey B, and Sweetie B the Bees

Confi the Conifer Tree and Mr. Tree

Franny Fish

Froggy

Lovey the Cat

Orchid and Daughter Minnie Orchid (Minnie O)

Rosie Flower

Squirrely

Ulog the Uncorruptible Lamb of God

Wiggly Worm

Woodsy the Woodpecker

Holy Day

"Live in each season as it passes. Breathe the air, drink the drink, taste the fruit, and resign yourself to the influences of each. Be blown on by all the winds."
Henry David Thoreau

On one particularly chilly day, Froggy's big, jeweled eyes open to the mesmerizing world of his critter friends and he sees that they are busy making preparations to celebrate the holiday, a holy day, each in their own way.

Mr. Tree's branches are filled with colors only seen once a year, while his best friend Confi, a tall, proud conifer tree, welcomes a swarm of light bugs to take a rest throughout their branches. Froggy knows that when the evening comes, those light bugs will bring a magical glow to his tree friends.

Franny Fish swims in the company of her brilliant schoolmates as they sing the songs of loving warmth and praises to the powers that be that they have spent all year practicing in their school.

Belle Birdie cannot be seen high up in the branches of her tree, but the aromas of what she's preparing float down to the pond, bringing joy and warmth to every creature along the way. Froggy's mouth waters as he thinks of the good foods he will be eating later at their get-together.

Orchid is moving her petals in a way she only does when she's in prayer. Rosie Flower is busy wrapping sweet little gifts for each of the creatures in and around the pond, which Bumbler B, Honey B, and Sweetie B have promised to deliver once she's finished.

Froggy and his critter friends rejoice in the season. In Froggy's world of plenty, everything needed to live well is right there. It's in the earth, in the waters, and in the air. It's everywhere.

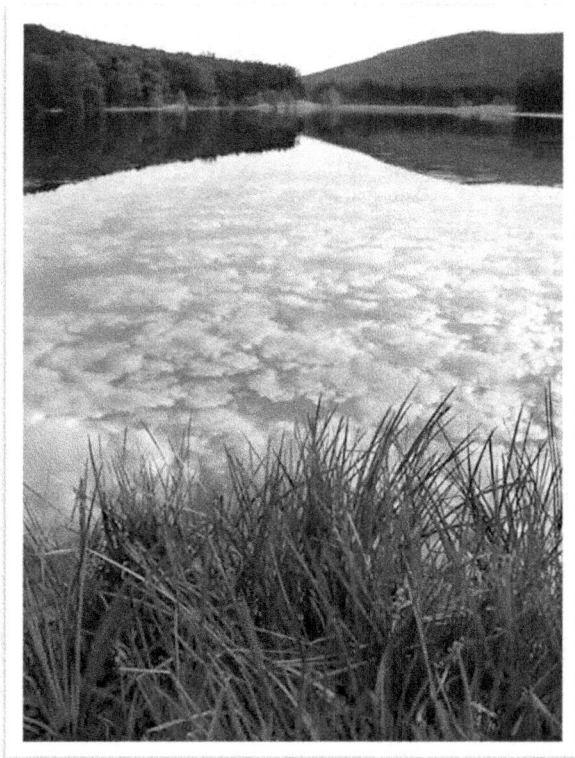

Baah, Baah, Baah

"God, I can push the grass apart
And lay my finger on Thy heart!"
Edna St. Vincent Millay

The Uncorruptible Lamb of God (Ulog) meets the critters and sees them in his likeness, pure, pristine, and perfect.

From Ulog's perspective, he views the skies above, the earth below, the waters that flow down nearby hillsides, the air that he breathes, the greenery that nourishes him. He is well pleased.

When Ulog greets a critter, he gives a baah, baah, baah that is mighty and powerful enough to be heard. He is saying, "Like me, you are a living expression of one who reigns on high."

At different times, each critter asks, "Ulog, can we see as you see? Can we live as you live? So often, we each have it so wrong. Every critter needs a tune-up, an adjustment, a course correction. What do you advise?"

To sum it up, the response is to pause, stop, be silent, and breathe. Remain in this sacred space for a while, a while longer, and longer still. Doing so, an unexplainable gift arrives. One that surpasses a critter's understanding. Let this space prevail.

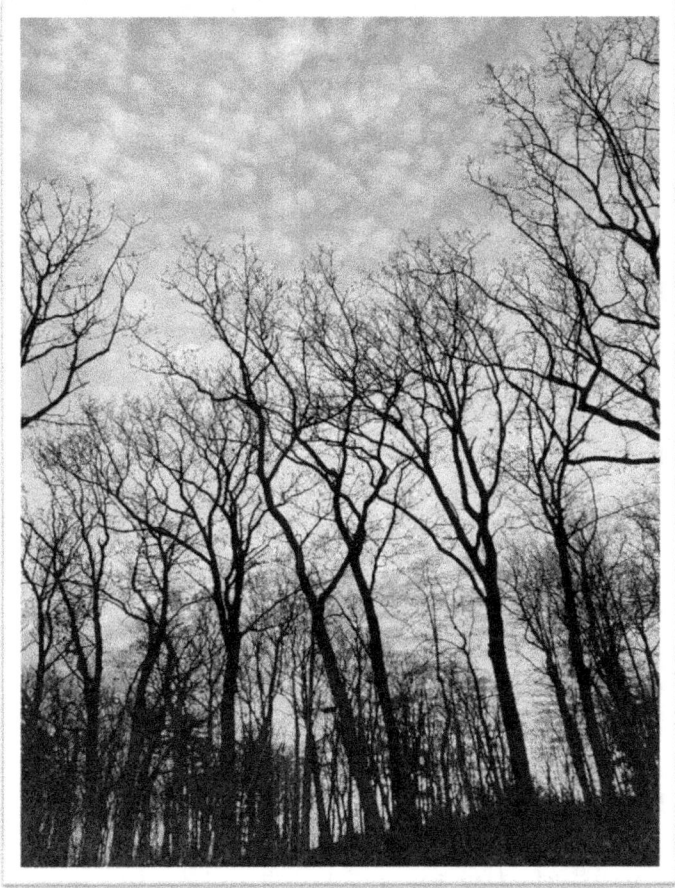

Harmony

*"The earth has its music for all
who will listen." Reginald Holmes*

Belle Birdie is in the birdbath. A splish here. A splash there. She is totally immersed in water that cleanses, refreshes, and invigorates. When she emerges, she flies to one of Mr. Tree's branches, where Bobalong Bird is weaving twigs and feathers into a nest.

"You're so busy," Belle says.

"Join me," Bobalog replies.

As they build together, their bird friends bring new supplies of dirt and mud, stems and leaves, straw and grass, and even a worm or two. Wiggly Worm is a good friend, so he remains free. While the birds tweet and twitter, Belle sings the sweetest and loveliest of songs. She is in harmony with all that surrounds her and more. On key, her music is transported afar.

During pauses, she listens, she waits. She hears the sounds of Ulog's footsteps in a distant pasture. In response, Belle's song has a bit of flourish. She has added some grace notes.

Bobalong hears the musical enhancement and asks, "To whom do you sing?"

"To the one who washed me in the birdbath, the same one who gave me a job to do, helping you build a nest, the very one who provided the twigs and other supplies, along with the many bird helpers."

Bobalong flaps his wings, acknowledging her response, and asks, "Why do you sing?'

"I sing to make music, especially when I see Mr. Tree and Confi grow new branches occupied by other nest builders and musicians. I love seeing the old and young branches pour forth fruits and nuts that fall to the ground for many to savor."

With that, Belle Birdie flew off into the distance to visit Ulog, grazing in the pasture.

Composure

"In the depths of winter, I finally learned that within me there lay an invincible summer."
Albert Camus

There goes Squirrely. Nervously running in circles on the ground, he scurries around. Squirrely goes this way and that way, up a tree, across a limb, and back down the tree. Always moving, always watching, Squirrely spies an acorn and buries it, only to dig it up later for a holiday treat. He repeats these antics endlessly. The hustle. The bustle. The frenzy.

Squirrely hears a rustling sound that comes from stepping on the season's fallen, crispy leaves. He stops all movement. He pauses and waits. He hears the clickety clack of gentle steps, crackling branches, and swishing blades of grass get louder. Whatever, whoever is making the sound is approaching.

A newcomer to this neighborhood, Squirrely lifts his eyes and sees a four-legged, curly-haired lamb. He sees Squirrely but remains composed, relaxed, and peaceful. That gives Squirrely comfort. The two acknowledge each other with a wink of the eye, a nod of the head.

Squirrely already likes this critter and asks the others if they have had the pleasure of making the lamb's acquaintance. He explains, "I met him when he calmed my endless frenzy, just with his presence."

Belle Birdie responds, "Oh, yes, that's Ulog." He's been here for three years. He baahs the sweetest sounds. Then I sing to the critters who are listening. They can tell you of his many gifts. Quite amazing, I must say."

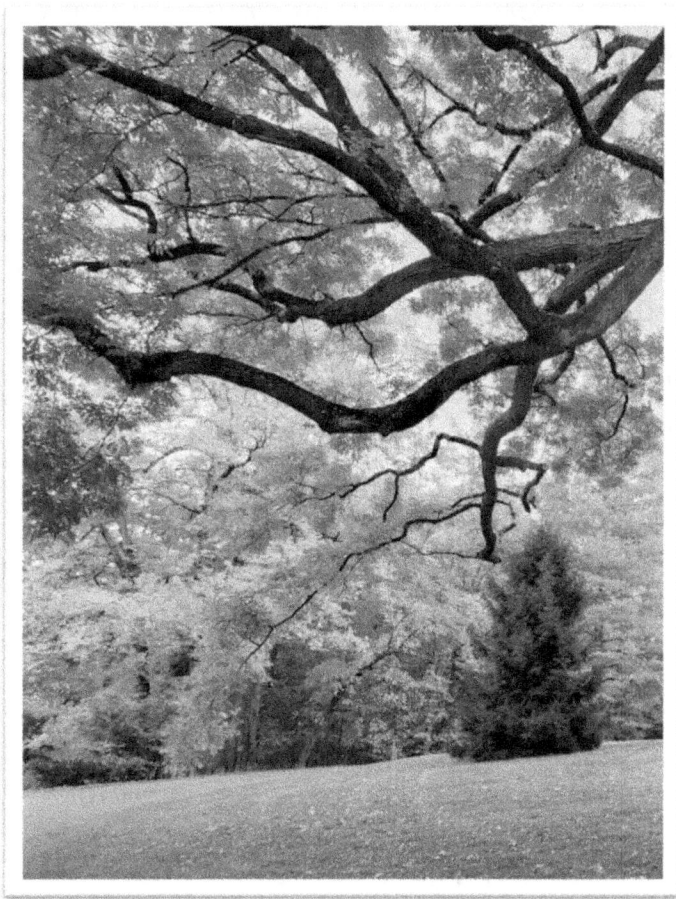

Ingredients

"Love the giver more than the gift." Brigham Young

As the critters planned their upcoming holiday feast, each considered what was available as ingredients for their cooking and baking.

An abundance of crops seemed to be everywhere. Apples and plums covered the branches of Mr. Tree. "I'm here for you. I'll shake my branches to let the fruits I pour forth fall to the ground. Take what you like," Mr. Tree said.

The neighboring nutty trees offered more contributions. "Come on over here and take what you like from our big walnut, oak, and pecan trees. Our branches are filled with hard shells, but don't be fooled. Tasty delicacies rest safely inside. You'll just need a nutcracker to get to them."

"Never mind that," said Woodsy with Belle Birdie and Bobalong Bird. "Our beaks can crack open the shells to uncover the hidden treasures within."

Confi pointed, "Over there's a maple tree dripping with sap, a sweet, thick syrup that coats what our two-legged visitors often serve for the holiday breakfast. So keep the sap flowing."

Orchid, Minnie O, Rosie Flower, and their blooming buddies joined in the conversation, "Over here. There's plenty of nectar and pollen." Bumbler B, Honey B, and Sweetie B buzzed right over to do their work for making honey, an ingredient for a favorite holiday dessert.

"Include us in the ingredients," the Chick Chick family added. "The eggs we lay, ones without chicks growing within, are a key ingredient in just about every dish served at the feast."

Ulog listened to the conversation, pleased at the generosity the critters and plants exhibited. He baahed in approval.

A Birth Day

"It's the beauty that thrills me with wonder, It's the stillness that fills me with peace."
Robert Service

Ulog was walking the pasture near Mr. Tree, hearing the songs of Belle Birdie, feeling the breeze, and witnessing the beauty of the blue sky above. He felt an obstruction underfoot, looked down, and saw an oval, brown egg with a bit of a crack. Ulog stopped, walked around it, and continued his walk.

A short distance away, he heard one crackle and then another, one peep and then another. Ulog turned around and saw the egg had changed. No longer content with a minuscule crack in the shell, something inside was poking it open. Ulog stood speechless. No baahs. He just watched silently as Baby Chick Chick emerged from the cracked shell. Other smooth-shelled eggs were nearby, likely ready to crack open and birth more Baby Chick Chicks.

Ulog wanted each Baby Chick Chick to emerge from the shell safe and sound, to grow into a loving hen like Mama Chick Chick or a powerful, crowing rooster like their Papa.

As he walked the pastures, Ulog told Squirrely and Froggy to watch their steps and be very careful to avoid an egg shell intended to give way to another Baby Chick Chick.

Ulog would often babysit for the young, not just Baby Chick Chick but Baby Squirrel, Baby Froggy, Baby Birdie, and other yet-to-be born babes. Each one loved Ulog. So did their parents, who copied Ulog's unparalleled baby rearing.

What a blessing to have Ulog on call.

A Work Day

"I do not at all understand the mystery of grace—only that it meets us where we are and does not leave us where it found us."
Anne Lamott

While Anty Annie is at work in the ant colony, she is busy building anthills, making tunnels, and carrying goods that keep her ant kin safe and sound.

Sometimes, other creeping, crawling critters visit. Right now, Wiggly Worm slithers by. Anty Annie greets Wiggly Worm but keeps him at a safe distance from some ants that like to feast on worms.

"To what do I owe the pleasure?" Anty Annie asks Wiggly Worm.

"Oh, the tunnels my wiggly friends have been burrowing are now traversing your tunnels. I wanted to stop by and thank you for doing such groundbreaking, foundational work."

"Thank you, too, Wiggly Worm. It's a pleasure to burrow into the earth and open passageways for water to trickle down to the roots of Orchid, Minnie O, and Rosie Flower, giving the hydration they need to grow and bloom."

"Bye for now, Anty. Until we meet again." Wiggly Worm slithers away. His visit is over, but his workday continues.

Both Anty Annie and Wiggly Worm help nourish and even embellish their habitat. You might say they grace the earth.

A distant Ulog takes in the fragrance of the nearby flowers and baahs in approval of their creation.

Charity

"Lord, make me an instrument of your peace...for it is in giving that one receives." Unknown

Mr. Tree often hears Woodsy chipping away on his bark. Mr. Tree, though, is not upset. His bark can withstand the chipping. You could say he is thick skinned. Mr. Tree is actually very pleased with visits from Woodsy, who regularly flies from critter to critter and knows all that is happening with each one. Then he shares some of the news with Mr. Tree. Woodsy is discreet. What should not be shared is kept in strict confidence.

On this particular day, Woodsy tells Mr. Tree about the holiday preparations. Belle Birdie and Bobalong Bird have gathered the other nearby birds to rehearse the carols often sung critter to critter, tree to tree, nest to nest, in the orchards, in the woods, on the earth, and even in the waterways. When the bubbles surface, Woodsy can hear how the swimmers grace the waters with gurgles of worship and praise.

Bumbler B, Honey B, and Sweetie B are preparing the honey that will be used in a honey cake. Trees in the orchard are bearing plums, apples, and nuts, ingredients that will go into recipes that the two-legged ones they see walking the grounds and swimming the waterways will use to prepare treats for the feast day. Orchid and Minnie O are of a species that blooms during this holiday season. They have their petals in prayer for a perfect day.

Woodsy is pleased again that, though this is a busy time for all, the critters are charitable and mindful of the reason for the season.

Play Time

"In November, the earth is growing quiet. It is making its bed, a winter bed for flowers and small creatures." Cynthia Rylant

Belle Birdie, Bobalong Bird, and Woodsy work hard and play hard. Their favorite game to play is "hold that pose" where they start sliding along the slippery rock padded with green fluff, then strike a pose, and see who can hold their pose the longest. Bobalong Bird once held a pose with one wing in the air so long he sank beneath the surface of the pond still holding his wing up.

Once the leaves start to fall, new slides open all around the pond. Half the fun is finding the new ones that nature has gifted them.

Bobalong Bird glides through the trees surrounding the pond one fine, crisp morning and spots a fallen branch. He travels to it to investigate. The branch appears to be secure in its position. He looks down the shaft and, through tiny breaks that let the light in, he sees the path straight down into a pile of leaves covered in a fresh coat of frost. He steps to the top of the branch and lets go, allowing gravity to work its magic.

Bobalong Bird rushes down the hollowed branch, stopping only when he lands in the snow and leaves. That was exhilarating.

He flaps back to Belle Birdie and Woodsy to let them know about the new slide. He's sure they'll be just as excited about it as he is.

Belle Birdie and Woodsy look down the fallen branch and then at one another. "I think we should try it," Belle Birdie says, more excited about the potential thrill than Woodsy is.

"After you," Woodsy offers, knowing it will take him a few moments to work up the courage to try this new slide.

"Alright, here I go," Belle Birdie smiles before jumping. Her scream startles Woodsy at first but calms him when it turns into a laugh as she lands with a thud in the leaves below. "Woodsy, you have to try this."

Strong-armed by his friends, Woodsy closes his eyes and steps into the hollowed branch. In less than a moment, he finds himself moving so fast he can't help but to scream. Before he knows it, his body is enveloped in cold leaves and his laughter joins the laughs of his friends.

"Ready to go again?" Bobalong Bird asks while bouncing.

"Yes," shouts Belle Birdie, ready to take off as soon as Woodsy answers.

"No, once was enough for me," Woodsy replies, "but play time has given me more energy to be here for others as Ulog always requests."

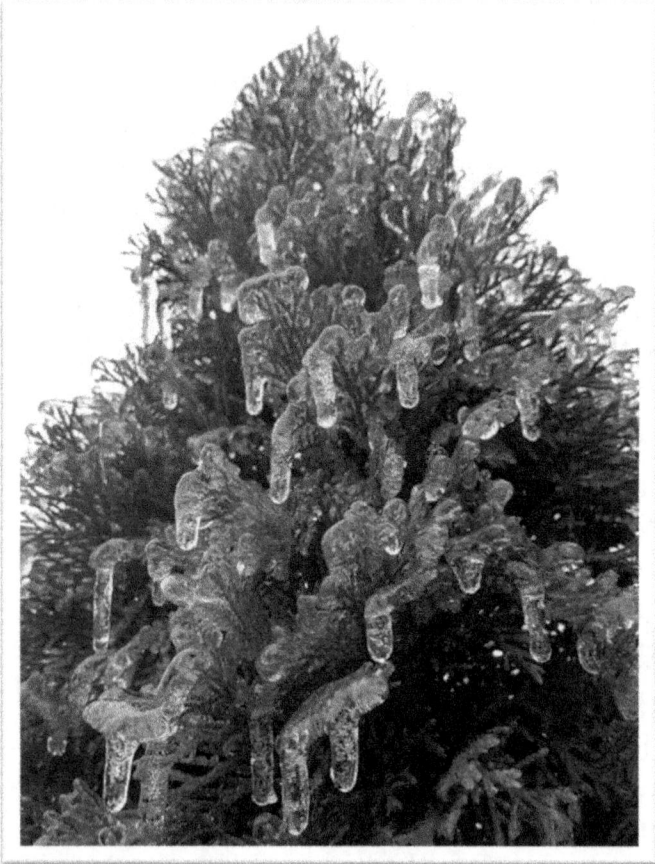

Fare Thee Well

"Blessed is the season which engages the whole world in a conspiracy of love."
Hamilton Wright Mabie

The winter solstice had just passed. Ulog could tell by the shortening of sunlit days, the lengthening of starry, darkened nights, and the ice and snow that covered the earth and topped the branches on Mr. Tree, Confi, and their forested kin. Ulog knew that the time had come to move on to greener pastures and asked Woodsy to convey this message and invite the critters to gather in the forest near Confi, who stood tall with branches aplenty. Each branch bore a decoration, a gift for Ulog. When all arrived, he asked, "What is this?"

Froggy started off the response. "Your presence in our midst means more than words can convey. Each branch that bears a gift is due to your guidance, your care, and yes, your love. With my every hop, skip, and jump, I could hear your baah of correction and your baah baah of approval."

Belle Birdie and Bobalong Bird added, "On flights to visit you, we often did not know where in the pasture you might be. It was easy for us to get lost. Then to the rescue you always came with a baah baah here and a baah baah there guiding our way to you."

Rosie Flower, Orchid, and Minnie O said, "With our petals in prayer, you provided sufficient sunshine and rain to blossom as you intended."

Bumbler B, Honey B, and Sweetie B had a few words. "How we appreciated your admonishment when we stung a fellow critter. We learned the importance of doing no harm."

Speaking of doing no harm, Anty Annie and Wiggly Worm added, "It's so easy for critters to step on our toes and ruin our monuments and passageways as well as many workers. You often stood watch, allowing others no approach."

Squirrely, always busy, busy, busy said, "From your gentle, peaceful stance and your measured baah, baah, baah, I paused for quiet moments to imbibe the aromas of the treats other critters are preparing for the feast and to listen to the music that the carolers are rehearsing."

One by one, each critter spoke.

With eyes that showed a tear here and there, Ulog had the final word. "You are never alone. Woodsy is here for you and knows how to reach me. Now enjoy the holiday. I'll see you again."

Purrs

"It is Christmas every time you let God love others through you."
Mother Teresa

Woodsy flew through the trees around the pond, scanning for sledding or sliding spots for him to enjoy with Belle Birdie and Bobalong Bird. The one Bobalong found was too intense for Woodsy's taste, so he is looking for an option more his speed.

As a woodpecker, he is used to moving fast when pecking the bark on a tree, but he is happy to go slow and steady, which is why he is gliding more than flying through the trees.

When he stops for a snack at the foot of his favorite oak tree, through the screen door in a brick structure that the two-legged creatures call home, Woodsy spots a critter inside. Fearing the critter is trapped, he flies as fast as he can to Froggy's stump.

"Froggy, I need your help. There's a critter trapped near my favorite snacking tree," Woodsy says once he catches his breath.

"Okay, let's see."

Woodsy leads Froggy to the oak tree. Froggy clears the croak in his throat and begins, "Woodsy, that structure is where the two-legged creatures, called humans, live."

"Is the critter their food? Is the critter trapped?"

The duo made their way through a metal gate and moved toward the place where Woodsy saw the critter. Inside the front door to the home sat a cat with large eyes and a flicking tail.

"Woodsy," Froggy began, moving his mouth as little as possible, "Don't make any quick movements. Cats take great pleasure in chasing birds and frogs."

"Oh Lovey, do you want to go outside?" a tiny voice from a young girl said from inside the home.

Lovey simply purred her response, "Yes."

The door opened, and Lovey the Cat walked toward Froggy and Woodsy.

With a serious look on her face, Lovey raised her paw toward Froggy and placed it on Froggy's nose. Then she broke out laughing.

Froggy and Woodsy looked at one another. "Is this normal for cats to do?" Woodsy asked. Froggy shrugged in response.

"You should have seen the looks on your faces." Lovey interrupted her laughter and wiped a paw against her eyes. "Hello, I'm Lovey the Cat. Nice to meet you," she offered her paw to Froggy to shake.

"Lovey?" Woodsy found his voice first.

"Yes, I came from a home with 14 other cats where only one of the humans knew our names. When she went away, another human took us to a different place where a team of people learned who we are and wrote our most distinguishing characteristic on our collars. I was the most loving cat, so I was gifted the name Lovey."

As Lovey spoke, Froggy and Woodsy relaxed. This cat just wants to tell them her story.

"Now I'm the only cat and I have five whole rooms in this home all to myself. I have a mom and a dad who take care of me and a little girl who feeds me well, even though the doctor told them I needed to be on a diet." Lovey whispers, "Fortunately for me, she's too young to know what a diet is, so she keeps scooping dry food into the bowl until it is overflowing." Lovey smiles.

"It sounds like you are very happy here," Froggy notes.

"Yes, but with that sacred holiday almost here, I am a bit puzzled. Mom says there's a legend that on Christmas Eve, cats gain the power to speak aloud to their humans. Is it true?" "Well, wait and see," answered Woodsy and Froggy.

Fast forward to Christmas Eve. The mom, the dad, and the little girl hear the purrs of Lovey in her cat language. Lovey moves toward them, snuggles very close, and with eyes open wide, she looks at the three of them. Then, in words she often hears the three humans speak to one another, Lovey whispers, "I love you." In awe, the mom, the dad, and the little girl pet Lovey.

What a glorious, magical Christmas Eve.

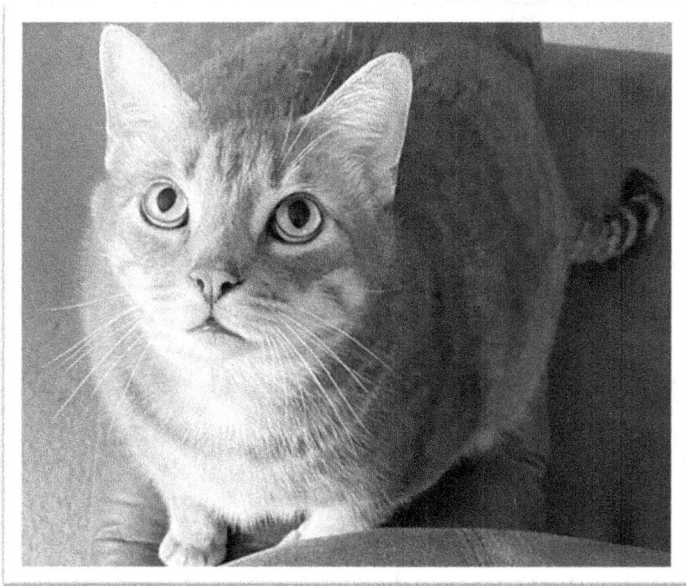

Hallelujah

"And the Grinch, with his Grinch-feet ice cold in the snow, stood puzzling and puzzling, how could it be so? It came without ribbons. It came without tags. It came without packages, boxes or bags. And he puzzled and puzzled 'till his puzzler was sore. Then the Grinch thought of something he hadn't before. What if Christmas, he thought, doesn't come from a store. What if Christmas, perhaps, means a little bit more." Dr. Seuss

On one particular day a while ago, Froggy found a wart, a slight imperfection, an irritant. Through a leap of faith, Froggy believed that this wart would be gone, gone, gone. That day arrives on Christmas Day as a miraculous gift.

Froggy's big, beautiful eyes are opened wide on the Christmas Day gathering of all the critters and he sees that they, too, are healed. Something has changed in each one of them. Mr. Tree no longer mourns the colorful leaves that have left his branches bare. In the sunlight, both old branches and new, baby branches now glisten and shimmer and sparkle with layers of glass-like crystal. Franny Fish no longer swims alone but enjoys the antics of her frolicking schoolmates.

Woodsy's aching back now is limber when flying to visit Belle Birdie perched high on an icy branch of Mr. Tree.

On this Christmas Day, Froggy and his critter friends rejoice and wonder, "What happened? Who or what is responsible for a life now free of warts, pain, and every kind of trial and tribulation?" From somewhere near Froggy's pond, they all hear now the muted "Baah. Baah. Baah" as Ulog journeys to his greener pasture. Their questions are answered.

This other worldly neighbor somehow knew what Froggy, Woodsy, Mr. Tree, Franny Fish, and Belle Birdie needed more than anything else.

Miraculously, Ulog had the power to make this Christmas Day the best one ever.

Hallelujah.

Easy Quiche

A note from Baby Chick Chick: While some eggs contain a Baby Chick Chick, many do not. We use these other eggs to make meals that are both delicious and nutritious. Two frozen pie shells often are packaged together. If you like, you can double this recipe with different crumbled ingredients in each Easy Quiche.

Half-bake one 9-in., deep-dish, frozen pie shell:

Line it with parchment paper or aluminum foil. To keep the crust from puffing up, fill the lined shell with pie weights or dry beans or rice (or use a fork to poke holes in the shell before lining it).

Bake at 375°F for 15 min. Then remove the liner and any weights and bake for about 5 min.

Mix and add to the pie shell:

1 ½ cups Swiss cheese

2 cups light cream

3 eggs, beaten

Add the following to suit your diet and taste:

> up to ¾ cup crumbled, cooked bacon, ham, salmon, crab, other meats, or vegetables

Bake at 375°F for 35 to 40 min. or until a toothpick comes out clean.

Chocolate Bark

A note from Squirrely: Trees do us all a great service by providing nuts and seeds—many more than are needed to support their own offspring and feed neighboring critters. These foods aren't just a foundation of our daily winter diet. They also add a lively crunch year-round. In this recipe, they add more texture and taste to an already-crunchy chocolate treat.

Place in a bowl and microwave for 2 min.:

> approximately 10 oz. dark chocolate chips with 72% cacao

Add to taste (a good heavy sprinkle):

> cinnamon

Spread a thin layer of melted chocolate onto a baking sheet covered with parchment paper. Then sprinkle with:

> kosher salt or sea salt
>
> nuts, chopped

Press down slightly on nuts with a spatula.

Refrigerate chocolate 20 to 30 min. until stiff.

Break chocolate into pieces and then keep them refrigerated.

Peanut Butter Fudge

A note from Froggy: I would like to thank my dear friend Squirrely for gathering the peanuts for me whenever I make this recipe. He also helps grind the nuts into a smooth peanut butter. It's important to wait for the milk and sugar to boil. Otherwise the sugar won't melt and the fudge comes out gritty.

Mix the following in a saucepan on medium heat and bring to a boil:

½ cup milk

2 cups sugar

Once the mixture is boiling and not just bubbling, stir for 2 ½ min.

Remove from the heat and stir in:

1 tsp vanilla extract

¾ cup peanut butter

Once the mixture is well-mixed and smooth, pour into a glass container.

Let harden for an hour. No refrigeration needed.

Slice and serve.

Apple Cake

A note from Mr. Tree: We love Apple Cake, courtesy of the trees in my orchard. Look for the many recipes for this favorite dessert, and be creative. Concoct an Apple Cake à la You. Thank you, Delicious, Granny Smith, and Macintosh for growing tasty apples.

Mix and add to a greased pie pan:

6 apples, sliced

¼ cup sugar

⅛ tsp cinnamon

⅛ tsp nutmeg

Bake at 350°F for 10 min.

In a small bowl, mix until smooth:

½ cup flour

½ tsp baking powder

⅛ tsp salt

½ tsp vanilla

1 egg

½ cup sugar

1 tbsp butter

Place the batter on top of the baked apples. Bake at 350°F for 30 min.

Honey Cake

A note from Sweetie B: Our whole family loves this Honey Cake. Though we don't know its origin, it's still a favorite at holiday gatherings. A big thank-you to Bumbler B and Honey B for collecting nectar and working their magic to make the yummy raw honey baked into this cake. How sweet it is to be busy bees and do such bee-autiful work.

In a large bowl, add in the order listed and then mix:

1 ¼ cups sugar

2 eggs

1 tsp allspice

1 cup honey

1 tsp baking soda

1 cup hot coffee

3 cups flour

1 tsp baking powder

½ cup salad oil

pinch of salt

dates (optional)

raisins (optional)

Place in a greased and floured 9 x 13 in.
pan or tube pan.

Top with:

½ cup walnuts, chopped

Bake at 300°F for an hr or until a
toothpick comes out clean.

Sugar Plums

A note from Belle Birdie: The toasting almonds and seeds fill my home with the scent of the holidays. When my baby birds are asleep for the night, my husband, Bobalong Bird, and I toast, mix, and enjoy these sugar plums, bringing the joy and excitement of the holiday season into our nest. The sugar plum mixture becomes quite sticky once the honey is added, so you are welcome to wear gloves if you don't wish to get your feathers dirty. The Sugar Plums are just as delicious if you skip the final roll in sugar. Enjoy.

Toast each in a pan on the stove for 5 to 7 min. on medium heat, giving each its own turn:

> 6 oz. slivered almonds (until they turn brown)
>
> ¼ tsp anise seeds
>
> ¼ tsp caraway seeds
>
> ¼ tsp fennel seeds

To create the fruit mixture, place the following into a food processor and pulse 20 to 25 times. Stop before the mixture turns into a ball.

> 6 oz. slivered almonds, toasted
>
> 4 oz. dried apricots

4 oz. dried figs

4 oz. dried plums

In a medium bowl, combine:

¼ cup powdered sugar

¼ tsp anise seeds, toasted

¼ tsp caraway seeds, toasted

¼ tsp fennel seeds, toasted

¼ tsp ground cardamom

pinch of kosher salt

Then add the following to the bowl and combine:

fruit mixture

¼ cup honey

Scoop sugar plum mixture into ¼ oz. portions and roll into balls. Set on a baking sheet with wax paper.

When ready to serve, roll a ball in sugar and enjoy.

1 cup coarse sugar

Authors

Judith Shenouda, author of four books, is owner of Shenouda Associates Inc., a business that researches, writes, and edits the many professional publications that streamline processes, launch products, and promote each client's brand.

Kerry Roberts is an adaptable writer with a flare for mathematics. With both sides of the brain at work, her writing is easy to digest.

Julia Ward is a versatile communicator who complements writing and editing with visual components.

This book, a collaborative effort of the technical and business communicators at Shenouda Associates Inc., is intended to show that our capabilities extend far beyond those of writing technical and business communications.

To learn more, visit

> https://easescommunication.com

Contact us at

> Shenouda@easescommunication.com